SPEED READING

- How to Read a Book a Day -

Simple Tricks to Explode Your Reading Speed and Comprehension

© Copyright 2017 by Ryan James - All rights reserved.

The following Book is reproduced below with the goal of providing information that is as accurate and as reliable as possible. Regardless, purchasing this Book can be seen as consent to the fact that both the publisher and the author of this book are in no way experts on the topics discussed within, and that any recommendations or suggestions made herein are for entertainment purposes only. Professionals should be consulted as needed before undertaking any of the action endorsed herein.

This declaration is deemed fair and valid by both the American Bar Association and the Committee of Publishers Association and is legally binding throughout the United States.

Furthermore, the transmission, duplication or reproduction of any of the following work, including precise information, will be considered an illegal act, irrespective whether it is done electronically or in print. The legality extends to creating a secondary or tertiary copy of the work or a recorded copy and is only allowed with express written consent of the Publisher. All additional rights are reserved.

The information in the following pages is broadly considered to be a truthful and accurate account of facts, and as such any inattention, use or misuse of the information in question by the reader will render any resulting actions solely under their purview. There are no scenarios in which the publisher or the original author of this work can be in any fashion deemed liable for any hardship or damages that may befall them after undertaking information described herein.

Additionally, the information found on the following pages is intended for informational purposes only and should thus be considered, universal. As befitting its nature, the information presented is without assurance regarding its continued validity or interim quality. Trademarks that mentioned are done without written consent and can in no way be considered an endorsement from the trademark holder.

Table of Contents

Introduction 1

Chapter 1: Understanding Speed Reading...............................5

Chapter 2: History of Speed Reading......................................10

Chapter 3: Reading vs Speed Reading 12

Chapter 4: What's Your Speed Reading Level? 16

Chapter 5: Debunking Myths about Speed Reading.........19

Chapter 6: Benefits of Speed Reading 22

Chapter 7: Breaking Poor Reading Habits 32

Chapter 8: Speed Technique: Make Your Eye Move Faster 43

Chapter 9: Comprehension Technique: Skimming+ 50

Chapter 10: Retention Technique: Maintain Focus 55

Chapter 11: Keys to Speed Reading Success 61

Chapter 12: Read a Book a Day - Speed Reading Exercises You Can Start and Make Into a Habit 64

Chapter 13: Speed Reading Tips that Enhance Your Habits..71

Chapter 14: Eye Exercises for Speed Reading.....................82

Conclusion 86

INTRODUCTION

Congratulations on purchasing the book, *"Speed Reading: How to Read a Book a Day - Simple Tricks to Explode Your Reading Speed and Comprehension"*.

Speed reading is the more efficient way to read and can bring you more benefits in life that you can ever imagine. You can go from good to great!

There are many misconceptions about speed reading that makes people apprehensive about learning this skill. But when you understand the benefits it can bring to your life, you will be more eager to learn how to do it. Speed reading will empower you, help maintain your focus, and increase your levels of comprehension.

You will be a more productive individual and still have time to enjoy other important things in life. Reading efficiently will allow you to acquire more knowledge which, in turn, makes you more creative, more innovative, and more successful.

Speed reading will give you the ability to read at least one book a day. Imagine how much information you can attain and retain! You can join the ranks of very successful people around the world who consider reading as an important tool to thrive in almost every area of life.

If you are already a reader, you will be surprised to know that speed reading will make that hobby a more enjoyable experience. It all starts with accepting that you may have poor reading habits that you need to get rid. This is so you can gain an understanding of speed reading techniques and how to apply them. In the following chapters, you learn more about how speed reading can work wonders for you.

It's never too late to learn a new skill. Start speed reading today!

Your Free Gift

As a way of saying thanks for your purchase, I wanted to offer you a free bonus E-book called *"How to Talk to Anyone: 50 Best Tips and Tricks to Build Instant Rapport"*.

Within this comprehensive guide, you will find information on:

- How to make a killer first impression
- Tips on becoming a great listener
- Using the FORM method for asking good questions
- Developing a great body language
- How to never run out of things to say
- Bonus chapters on Persuasion, Emotional Intelligence, and How to Analyze People

To grab your free bonus book just tap here, or go to:

http://ryanjames.successpublishing.club/freebonus/

CHAPTER 1

UNDERSTANDING SPEED READING

A lot of people don't realize that reading is a skill that they often use. You read the news on paper or on the internet to see what's happening around you. You read books, letters, social media posts, recipes, and all kinds of notes during an average day. You read financial reports and business correspondence. You browse numerous emails from friends or colleagues at work. Do you realize how much reading you actually get done in one day?

You may think that it is enough knowing how to read and comprehend. But even if you are able to do the basics well, you can still improve your reading skill – and you should, since reading takes up a lot of time in your everyday life. Poor reading habits can be changed and unlearned to make you more efficient and more productive. This is where *speed reading* comes in.

Did you know that the average person can read approximately 200 to 250 words in a minute, or take about 2 minutes to read a page of a document? With speed reading, you can actually double your reading rate of words/minute. You can breeze through, and comprehend, any content in half the time! Imagine what you can do with the time you save! You can use it to complete other tasks, or just rest and relax.

The art of speed reading improves your comprehension skill by allowing you to have a "bigger picture" grasp of what you are reading. As a skill, this can be advantageous to your work or profession.

The Science of Reading

Before you proceed to mastering speed reading, you must first understand the way you read. Reading is a complex skill. Different people have different ways on how they make sense of letters and how they are put together. It is not true that you need both of your eyes to be focused on a specific letter within a word. Each eye can actually focus on different letters simultaneously, normally two characters away from each other. Your brain puts these images together and constructs the word. This process happens in an instant, so a reader can actually zip through many different texts at a given time.

There are many different categories of reading and these affect how fast a person reads. Before you get to speed reading, you have to understand that every person is wired differently based on how they were taught as well as other influences surrounding them. Typically, people learn to read when they begin school and they are commonly taught to do so word by word. Word by word reading causes the eyes to be fixated on only one word, sometimes the previous one, taking the reader back a step in reading and comprehension. This mechanical form of reading is rather slow, but this is the most common way through which people read and comprehend. Not everyone is informed that there is a more efficient way.

When you think about how much time is spent just looking at several words and concepts, reading may seem like a tedious and very mechanical process. There is *fixation* – basically staring at a word or a couple of words which usually takes a quarter of a second. Then one's eye will move to another word or set of words, the process is called *saccade*, and it takes a tenth of a second. Then the reader repeats the cycle and pauses about half a second to comprehend what he or she just read. These mechanical processes put together become the reason why an average person can read about only 200 to 250 words a minute.

The different types of reading are:

- *Mental reading*

- *Auditory reading*

- *Visual reading.*

Mental reading is also known as sub-vocalization. It is a way of reading wherein one sounds out every word internally, much similar to saying something to yourself. Mental reading is the slowest type of reading. Readers who practice mental reading can read to about 250 words a minute.

Auditory reading is a bit faster, as it requires the person to listen to every word that is read and not sound them out. Those who practice this usually read 450 words a minute.

The fastest type is visual reading. Instead of sounding out the words or hearing them, the reader comprehends what the word means by sight, making them read an average of 700 words a minute. Speed reading via visual reading is a skill you can master as you continually practice and train.

Now, speed reading can be very handy and valuable. However, it is safe to say that there are instances when using speed reading is not a good idea. There are reading materials that you should never speed read. You must know when and how to adapt a reading technique according to the material on hand.

In the following chapters you will discover the benefits of speed reading, its history and comparison to average reading as well as on how to develop and master speed reading so you can use it to your advantage.

CHAPTER 2

HISTORY OF SPEED READING

It is good to understand how the concept of speed reading came about. The beginnings of speed reading was created through the use of the *tachistoscope*, a device used by the US Air Force to train their pilots' focus and memory. The gadget will show the pilot an image for a short period of time then remove it from view. The pilot would have to identify which are enemy planes while they simulate battles in the cockpit.

This *tachistoscope* methodology was later applied to reading: it flashed a group of words on a screen for .002 seconds and readers were tested if they remembered and understood the phrase completely.

In the beginning, it was believed that people read by looking at all the letters in a word then associating them with meaning. The concept of "reading by letters" was changed when it was proved, through studies and experiments, that people have the ability to read not just one word, but a group of three, five, or even more words at a given time. Thus, speed reading was popularized.

Evelyn Wood was the one who coined the phrase. She studied the habits exhibited by fast readers and developed techniques on how to enhance one's reading speed. She taught in schools and seminars. President John F. Kennedy, along with his brother Bobby, was schooled in her methods and became a strong advocate for speed reading during his term. President Jimmy Carter, his wife, and several White House staff similarly took speed reading courses.

Through the years, speed reading methodologies have been upgraded. However, the basic foundation – reading multiple words faster and with full comprehension – has not changed. You can apply latest developments in speed reading to go from being a good reader to becoming a great one.

CHAPTER 3

READING VS SPEED READING

The skill of speed reading is not very different from average reading – the only thing is that it is a lot more focused. Average reading requires you to engage your senses (sight, hearing, speaking) and your brain. With speed reading, you need to utilize your brain power and these senses in even greater fashion so that you will be more focused and more efficient.

Here's how speed reading expands the natural way of reading:

1. **You *see* the words.**

   Initially you read a group of words (usually 3 to 5) at a glance. If they are words that you are familiar with, you don't have to read them one by one. Next, you magnify your vision and try to read and comprehend more words at a glance. Many well-practiced speed readers can easily see and process about 10 to 16 words. Then you magnify your vision to read line by line, horizontally and vertically, per page. Most good speed readers can easily see and process about 2 to 3 lines at once.

2. **You do *silent reading*.**

Average readers sound out words as they read. This is okay for beginners but if you want to speed up, you will have to do away with it. Speed readers can read without the voice (not even a whisper in their mind) and just use their eyes and brain.

3. **You *decode* the words.**

The mind decodes words that you fail to recognize. It breaks the words into syllables and tries to get the meaning then pronounce it. When you don't know what it means, you check the dictionary. An average reader will take a much longer time to read when they encounter unfamiliar words. As you read more material, you are introduced to more new words. You will eventually increase your speed reading rate whilst you also continue to expand your vocabulary. You will find it easier to decode words after that.

4. **You *comprehend* the material.**

Learning something and understanding it is the purpose of reading. It is not just seeing letters, words, phrases or sentences put together – it's about getting the whole thought, obtaining information and probably gaining new perspective. When it comes to speed reading, the level of your comprehension can be determined by the following concentration, extensiveness of your vocabulary, background of the subject matter, and reading speed.

<u>Concentration:</u> Whenever you read, you need to have concentration. Speed reading would require double the average amount of concentration you put into reading text. Your focus needs to be sustained because you see, decode and comprehend all at the same time and do so within a small amount of time. You need to be attentive to the main ideas so you can get a good grasp of your material.

Extensiveness of vocabulary: When you have a wide vocabulary, you will find it easier to understand the material you are reading. You will not have to stop and try to properly understand the meaning of a word or words from other sources. You can use your time to finish reading more material.

Background of subject matter: When you are already familiar with the material you are reading, you will have a head start with comprehending it fully – you understand key points, you get the jargon and style, and you know the main points to look for.

Reading speed: It is not just about reading fast – it is about reading wisely. It's all about perspective: a speed reader knows when they need to speed up and when they need to slow down and take his time. They would also know when to skim and when to focus more on weighty concepts. It depends on the type of reading and the material that they are reading. Not reading at the right speed will weaken your comprehension.

CHAPTER 4

WHAT'S YOUR SPEED READING LEVEL?

Before you begin to apply speed reading techniques, you need to know where you are right now as a speed reader. As with learning or trying out anything new, you need to make an honest evaluation of yourself so that you know where you must start and which areas you have to work on.

Readers fall into different categories based on how fast they read counted in *words per minute* (wpm). Find out what level speed reader you are:

IF YOU READ 1 To 200 WORDS PER MINUTE,

You are very likely a TALKER (translated: SLOW READER). This means that you read words at the same speed as you speak. Talkers usually practice sub-vocalization – you may even find yourself moving your lips as you read. Talking back or sounding out holds you back because you are hearing your voice in your head and you can't go any faster than the way you talk.

IF YOU READ 200 to 300 WORDS PER MINUTE,

You are considered an AVERAGE READER. You only probably read when you have to, and you won't take up reading as a hobby. While you are faster than a talker, since you can read a group of words at once, you may also be practicing vocalization. A lot of people are at this level.

IF YOU READ 300 to 700 WORDS PER MINUTE,

Consider yourself an ABOVE AVERAGE READER. You are someone who rarely vocalizes and you can read chunks of words at a glance while completely understanding the material. It is highly likely that your vocabulary is wide and you enjoy doing a lot of reading.

IF YOU READ MORE THAN 700 WORDS PER MINUTE,

You are a SPEED READER! You find yourself reading more than 10 words at a glance. You can read both vertically and horizontally without much problem. You have great comprehension. You not only enjoy reading, but you are very confident about your skill.

If you can read up to 16 words in one look and fully comprehend it, then you are a speed reader who doesn't need lessons at all. If you are a struggling reader, and you want to get better then read on. You will get practical tips on how to increase your level of speed and comprehension. If you are either average or above average, this book will help you enhance your skills further so that you can easily become a speed reader!

CHAPTER 5

DEBUNKING MYTHS ABOUT SPEED READING

There are many misconceptions about speed reading and when you don't set things straight, you will have a harder time working on your level and improving your speed rate. After all, one reason for learning speed reading should be to bring enhancement to your reading ability as well as making reading a pleasurable and profitable experience for yourself.

You may think you have an idea of speed reading – and these ideas may not be right at all! It's perfectly normal. A lot of people have erroneous concepts of how to read fast and most of them are untrue.

Read on and find out the wrong ideas people have about speed reading. You don't have to be stuck with these myths. All you have to understand is that you only need to make slight adjustments to your established routines and habits, and you will be well on your way to becoming a speed reader.

- *Myth 1*

When you speed read, you don't enjoy reading.

This is false because speed reading actually allows you to read more efficiently. And when you read more efficiently – you not only save time, you also understand more! This means you get to enjoy reading more books, magazines, articles, blogs and other reading materials, print or online. A lot of people also pick up a love for reading once they learn how to speed read.

- *Myth 2*

When you speed read, you don't have to understand as well and as much as average reading.

This is untrue since speed reading requires a higher level of focus. When you concentrate well, you will also comprehend things better. With speed reading, you are able to read in context and understand better in the least amount of time.

- *<u>Myth 3</u>*

When you speed read, you skip words.

You don't skip anything when you speed read, the difference is that you no longer read the text word by word. Speed reading makes you read words in chunks or by line so you don't fixate your eyes on just one. You will understand faster when you read more words by line. But you don't miss out on any word.

- *<u>Myth 4</u>*

When you speed read, you need to move your finger across the text.

A guide or a pacer is a helpful tool when you begin to learn speed reading. You use it to mark where you are on the page to prevent regression and help you keep focus. You will learn more about meta guiding or using pacers in the succeeding chapters.

However, keep in mind that not all speed readers keep their fingers or a pencil as they go through pages quickly. Once you get the hang of it, you will be able to drop the pacer and speed read with ease.

CHAPTER 6

BENEFITS OF SPEED READING

Speed reading offers plenty of benefits for everyone, this is especially so for business people, students, and for anyone who does a lot of reading.

You may be wondering why it is beneficial to spend time learning speed reading techniques despite your day being already full. Here's one reason: With the vast amount of information coming at you every day, investing a little time in learning strategies for faster reading makes sense.

Imagine zipping through your email inbox in half the time, efficiently going through the social media updates of your friends and responding quickly.

Speed reading is a technique that will allow you to comprehend more and increase the rate of your reading to double or even triple that of your current level. Once you acquire the ability, you will have the skill for life and enjoy its long-term benefits! Isn't that a sweet deal?

Here are some more reasons that will help you decide to start learning and improving on your speed reading skills:

1. **You will have develop better time management.**

   The old adage *time is* gold is so true. Everyone should use their time wisely because it is the most precious commodity you will ever have. Success largely depends on how you manage your time. With speed reading, you can save up time going through different materials to gain useful information and use that time to apply that knowledge you gained.

2. **You will be empowered.**

   First impressions and judgments are usually based on the words that leave a person's mouth. For example, being able to share your point of view or understanding of important facts in a business meeting will not only give you a boost of confidence but also a chance to impress other people with your knowledge. Having been able to speed read through pertinent documents (reading AND fully comprehending the contents) will give you knowledge power.

Another instance would be social situations. Having sped read news – whether it's about world events, social media, industry, entertainment, or even gossip – you will be able to hold conversations better with others and be comfortable with what you know.

3. **You will be exposed to more opportunities.**

Exponential growth comes as you read more and expand your knowledge. And as your speed reading improves, you will gain even more wisdom that will help you grow professionally and personally. This will open the door for many opportunities that you can take hold of.

Did you know that speed reading can help you get promoted or get you that high-paying job you have been eyeing? In today's competitive corporate world, you can stand out by getting advanced degrees, formal trainings or certifications. You can do these things online and speed reading can help you improve your educational background by managing these courses and accomplishing them in a shorter amount of time with great results.

Remember, when you increase your professional value, it translates to better opportunities for employment and income. This equates to more security and financial freedom.

4. **You become more confident.**

Speed reading can improve or strengthen your personality. If you are a person who is not comfortable speaking to colleagues or your boss, you will stay in the sidelines and have no confidence to really participate. However, if you keep abreast of what is happening within and around your company and industry, you will be able to make confident suggestions and proposals.

You can speed read through financial news, industry updates, and reports on what is going around the competition in the marketplace. You will also be able to answer questions confidently.

Even when people disagree with your opinion, you will be comfortable and confident knowing that you have full comprehension of the topics you are discussing because you have read them well– through speed reading.

With improved self-confidence, you're also better at exercising self-control and make wiser decisions in the workplace.

5. **You will have better memory.**

A lot of people can read through something and forget what they have read after a while. Speed reading techniques can increase your understanding of a topic or fact that you have come across. Your brain is wired to recall, with precision, concepts that you have good comprehension of. You can make your brain stronger and more efficient by training it through speed reading. When you improve your memory, you will also improve on your creativity.

6. **You will feel more relaxed.**

People who read will tell you that it can be a very relaxing, stress-busting pastime. Whether you read slow or read fast, reading can relax your nerves and ease the worries out of your thoughts. Picking up and going through the right book at the right time can instantly change your mood or your whole perspective about a subject.

As you speed read, you will be able to go cover more material, absorb more information and generally feel more relaxed. In doing so, you will also be able to quiet the voices, noise and tension around you. This peaceful state can enhance your emotional and spiritual being, which brings positive results to your physical body.

Try speed reading for a month and you will begin to see a marked difference in your behavior and emotions.

7. **You will enhance your learning capabilities.**

Speed reading is a way to enhance your focus. When you know how to give your full concentration on whatever task you are doing, you will get better at it – this applies not just to reading. You will have more interest on what you are doing and you can process information better and at a much faster rate. You will also be eager to grab at any chance to enhance your learning and creativity. Again, this paves the way to more opportunities.

8. **You will be more sophisticated with your thinking.**

   Science says that speed reading can positively affect the brain's neuroplasticity. The brain will be trained to chart new connections and allow you to think in a more complex and advanced manner.

9. **You will have less stress.**

   Since speed reading trains you to focus, through it you would be able to increase your meditation skills. In today's world of information overload, people tend to multi-task and lose focus. Fragmented attention will make you inefficient and unproductive. Not getting tasks done, or attending to too many tasks at once, will bring you stress.

   When you learn to focus, a skill acquired through speed reading, you will be able to complete tasks more efficiently and have much less stress because you know you're performing at your best.

10. You will be inspired to achieve or dream more.

With enhanced memory, focus, thinking, and creativity, you will find yourself aspiring for more. As the world around you becomes bigger, you will dare to dream bigger and go further. The benefits of speed reading skills are not limited to just reading and comprehension. It can affect your whole outlook in life.

11. You will be more innovative as a leader.

Speed reading can enhance your thought processes and make you a better leader. As a leader, you would be able to lead changes, expansion, and innovation confidently knowing that you have the right information and the skills to meet the goals you set.

You also become more creative at problem-solving as you engage your imagination. You can cross-pollinate concepts and make them more useful. You have the skill to implement the initiative as well. Who knows, the next billion-dollar idea may just come from you.

12. You become good at problem-solving.

Speed reading allows you to reframe problems by understanding key ideas and unlocking your imagination. Did you know that your subconscious is powerful? Studies indicate that the subconscious mind solves problems at 100,000 mph while the conscious mind can only go at a maximum of 150 mph.

How does speed reading help you solve problems faster? Speed reading gives you the skill to course more facts and figures to your subconscious. When the subconscious has more information, it can solve problems better. This is called logic training. When you speed read, you train your brain to be more efficient at receiving and understanding new information then connecting it to what is previously stored.

You will have enhanced logical thinking processes as you continue to enhance your speed reading since the connections that are needed for it gets activated. You will see the benefits of these enhancements to your thinking process in your everyday decision-making.

CHAPTER 7

BREAKING POOR READING HABITS

As with developing other new skills, learning speed reading will require you to unlearn and break old reading habits that you have acquired over the years. You cannot become a speed reader when you still practice poor reading habits.

It is common for people to have one or two, or even more, poor or slow reading habits. When these habits are done away with, a person can make room for new and efficient habits in their life. First, you will need to understand the most common poor reading habits, see if you are practicing them, and learn what you can do to overcome them.

Remember, the goal of learning to read fast is more than just speed – it is to become more efficient at reading and comprehension.

1. **Sub-Vocalization**

    As you learned in the early chapters, young readers were trained to pronounce every word in their heads or mutter under their breaths while they read. As they grew older, they began to develop an "inner monologue" going on in their minds whenever they read—this happens as a force of habit. Their reading speed is similar to how fast they talk. While it is conventional, sub-vocalization prevents a person from improving his reading speed.

    Here is how sub-vocalizing can slow you down: the average talking rate of a person is 200 to 250 words per minute. When you sub-vocalize, you read at the same speed. While you have been previously trained to do so, you don't have to say or hear every word in your head in order to understand what you are reading.

    When you train yourself to speed read, your mind can automatically process what you see so you don't have to stop and sound it out. You can improve your reading speed from the normal

200 to 250 words a minute to just about any level you decide.

In order to overcome this poor reading habit, *honesty is key*: you need to acknowledge that you actually have a voice in your head and that you should turn it off when reading. The next step is to practice not speaking. Here are some tips on how to stop "saying or hearing words as you read" and kick that bad habit out of your life:

- *Don't read for sound.* This means that you read for meaning. It is a lot like listening. You hear words – but the voice is not yours – and your brain makes the connection of what the speaker (in this case, the author) is trying to send across. Listening while reading means you are reading for meaning. You are not looking for the sound so the words that you see are read as units of meaning.

- *Stop those lips from moving.* Chew gum so that your mouth has something to do other than sound out the words as you see them. By disengaging your vocal system, you will be able to "listen" and get the message without vocalizing what you see.

- *Quiet the inner reading voice.* This may take a bit of work but when you train yourself to do so, you will soon find yourself speed reading with ease. Perceive words instead of seeing them. Think of words as symbols instead of sound.

- *Take in more words.* When you widen what you see, you are making yourself read more words and your brain stops vocalizing. Speed reading is all about focus. Concentrate hard and find thought units and not words in sentences.

2. Word-by-Word Reading

This is about focusing on reading separate words instead of ideas. You can get the gist of a phrase or sentence in groups of words instead of taking it one by one. This makes comprehension difficult and people read even more slowly. The best way to break this habit is to learn how to properly chunk words together and get what they mean as a block. Look at this simple sentence: *Time is gold*. Did you read it word for word or as an idea? You can increase your vision span to absorb in more words and still understand the concept.

Creating blocks of words, also called "word-chunking", is a way to eliminate sub-vocalization. Chunking means you train your eyes to read a set of words at once. This way, you read faster. Try reading the following: *The quick brown fox jumps over the lazy dog.* You can read it in blocks or phrases at a glance as: *the quick brown fox | jumps over | the lazy dog* by focusing on the words fox, jumps and dog. Overall, you understood what the sentence meant. When you read in chunks, you will cover more text, thus read faster.

You can take chunking up a notch by separating sentences or paragraphs and reading them by sections. Read one block as one concept, and do this for the rest of the page. After you're done you'll realize that you have read through the whole page faster. This exercise will take practice so challenge yourself to do it often until you feel comfortable and confident with it.

3. **Ineffective Eye Motion**

   As with reading word by word, when you don't use your peripheral vision to work your way across the text, you will be a slow reader. When your eyes are not trained to take in a lot of words or a whole line of text, you will read ineffectively.

   Normally, your eye can see about an inch-and-a-half at a time – this means that it is possible to view up to five words at a glance. To overcome ineffective eye motion, you need to relax and expand your gaze. By doing so, you will not see a single word specifically, but blocks of words that hold meaning. Using your peripheral vision is the level that comes after chunking – reading a whole line instead of a small group of words.

   To do this, you need to focus on the middle first then scan the rest of the line using your peripheral vision. Don't worry too much that you will skip a word – you won't. As you go through your material using this method, you will realize that you will cover more text and still understand everything you just read.

Remember that like other speed reading techniques, this will take practice, but you will be happy with the results. Learn more about improved eye fixations and how you can exercise your eye muscles in chapter 9 of this book.

4. Regression

Skipping back to the words you have already read is called regression. This is a common practice of slow readers. When you worry about forgetting or misunderstanding a text then go back to read it again, you will most likely lose your focus and your reading flow.

When you regress, there is the danger of losing your comprehension of the whole subject. Re-reading can be counter-productive. Instead of flitting back and forth, train yourself to read in one smooth flow. You must be aware of this: only re-read the text when you absolutely need to. Otherwise, just proceed.

You can also be subconsciously regressing and wasting time. To avoid re-reading or reduce the amount of time you regress you can use a guide or pointer. As you move the pointer across the page, your eyes will naturally follow along. You will train your eyes to dodge skipping back and just follow the pointer. You can use your finger as a pointer.

Practice doing this so you can force yourself to not stop or go back. When you reach the end of your page, think about what you read. When you recall what you have just finished reading, without going back, it's a good start. Continue to practice reading this way until you get to the point that you don't have to use a pointer.

5. **Poor Concentration**

    Here's a fact: poor concentration does not produce good results. When you try to read while watching television, you will find it hard to focus on reading. Even if you learn to turn off sub-vocalization and read by chunks, you will not have full comprehension with poor focus. Without concentration, the words will blur into each other.

If you want to be able to read fast and comprehend well, take away as much distraction as you can. Set up a conducive reading environment. Try to avoid multitasking as you read.

Distractions are not just external – there are also internal distractions such as going over events of the day in your mind or thinking about what to do next. Allowing your thoughts to wander will restrain your ability to comprehend. Go to *chapters 11 and 12* for tips on how to create the right reading environment that is essential to building your speed reading skills.

6. Practicing linear reading

The traditional linear reading is what most readers are trained to do: to read from left to right, across to down, from beginning to end. Non-linear reading is a reading technique that allows you to jump from one section to another, oftentimes not actually finishing a sequence.

While linear reading is acceptable, it could also mean that you are wasting time by paying attention to supplemental information. You can overcome this poor reading habit by doing things non-linearly.

The first thing you should do is search for the following: headlines, bullet points, headings, items in boldface/highlight and transitions. You can scan the contents quickly and identify what is important and what is supplemental. Don't waste time on fluff, but find key information.

Look for interesting and engaging points that authors usually put in – this will help you understand the point that the writer is trying to get across, so you don't have to go through the anecdotes, stories or accompanying examples that expand their concept.

You can choose to re-read or skip parts that you like. You can learn how to skim more effectively in chapter 10.

7. **Not knowing how to skim**

Skimming can be handy when it is crunch-time. When the teacher suddenly calls for a recitation or a pop quiz but you forgot to read through your lesson yesterday, or when your boss calls for a meeting and you only have 10 minutes to read through the reports, you need your speed reading skills.

You waste precious time and you don't get the necessary information when you don't know how to skim. Calm down, take a breath, open that book or report and read through it the right way. The key is to find the main points or headlines. You can go through the headings or the table of contents, then subtitles or captions. This will give you an overall feel of what the whole document or chapter is about.

After you go through the headings, read through the first paragraph, the last one and the middle part. Piece together what you got and when you have an idea, you can start reading the rest, if you still have time. This process will allow you to keep information better. There is a chapter in this book dedicated to skimming.

CHAPTER 8

SPEED TECHNIQUE: MAKE YOUR EYE MOVE FASTER

A speed reader has greater comprehension when they read in chunks or phrases since there is stronger meaning conveyed. The eyes need to be still and focus in order to see something. When the eyes are moving around, the vision will be blurry. Speed reading is not just about moving your eyes quickly across the page, it is about having good focus while maintaining a wide span of vision.

It is also about improving fixation: how the eyes move and become still as you read, how it focuses on a group of words then proceed to the next after understanding the first one. The fewer fixations, the faster reading.

To understand how eyes fixate itself on words, try to read this:

A thing of beauty is a joy forever.

If you are a slow reader, you will read this sentence in 5 to 8 eye fixations – as your eyes go word by word. When you are a fast reader, you will have greater span of vision and be able to read this in two or four eye fixations only.

A *thing* | of *beauty* | is a *joy* | *forever*.

A thing of *beauty* | is a *joy* forever.

If you want to see how eye fixation works in action, you can ask a friend to observe you while you are reading or you can observe him. You will notice that the reader's eye will move from left to right in a fraction of a second then move again to the right. Once the reader gets to the end of the line, his eyes will go back to the left and start fixations all over again. Eye fixations vary depending on the length of the line he is reading, his familiarity with the subject and the breadth of his vocabulary.

Eye Fixations and Familiarity

Your background, education, and interest all factor into your rate of speed reading. Your knowledge of a topic will influence how fast you read per eye fixation. Reading about something that is in your field of expertise will allow you to read not just quickly but confidently. You are aware of jargon and the topic of interest. Compared to a grade-schooler, a finance consultant will read a business report or an investment proposal much faster and understand it better.

As you read and read, you will expand your knowledge. As you become familiar with more and more topics, you will read even faster. It works and benefits you both ways.

Eye Fixations and Vocabulary

The wider your vocabulary, the greater your word recognition will be as you read. This means you can take in more words in groups. Here is a good example of having limited vocabulary. Read the following and try to comprehend what the author is saying: *Sownynge in moral vertu was his speche, and gladly wolde he lerne, and gladly teche.*

This text is from The Canterbury Tales. When you are not familiar with these words, you will notice that it took you a longer amount of time to read it (you tried to read and understand it word by word) compared to reading this:

Filled with moral virtue was his speech, and gladly would he learn, and gladly teach.

When you expand your vocabulary, you will be able to read faster (in groups of words) because you don't have to take time to think what the words mean. Your brain has already processed it from memory. When you read more, you will encounter new words and you will learn more, thereby widening your vocabulary.

Practice Meta Guiding

Again, remember that the eyes have the habit of becoming fixated on objects that move. For instance, if you are sitting in front of the television, and a cockroach flies on your side, you will automatically focus on it. Or if you were talking to someone and a ball is suddenly thrown your way, you will naturally look towards it and react quickly. Eye fixation is a reflex that you should use to your advantage.

When you read, the words aren't moving but you can use your fingers or any kind of pointer so that your eyes will follow it. This is often referred to as meta guiding. It is an old technique that eliminates distractions and allows the reader to focus on important words so they can read faster.

Since the eyes are naturally attracted to movement, using a guide helps the reader expand their peripheral vision and be able to read multiple lines as guided. Using a guide helps control and improve eye fixations. It also gives the reader a way of navigating the layout and organization of the text, becoming more aware of headings and bolded texts, as well as looking for the ways in which the author transitions from one topic to the next.

As you use your guide, you can also regulate your speed so that you can go fast or slow as needed. Practice it and identify how much you can read in a minute. Keep on practicing and after a while, reading with the flow of your guide will come naturally and you will read smoothly.

Once you get better at speed reading, you can do away with your guide and your eyes will naturally move smoothly over the material.

You can read in increments in 1 to 5 minutes to track your progress. If you want to get an average of your speed rate (words per minute), count the number of lines you can read in a minute then multiply by ten – you use 10 because it is the average number of words per line in printed books. Every time you practice speed reading, make it a goal to beat your previous score. You will soon find yourself going faster.

Rapid Serial Visual Presentation

It has been established that when you make fewer eye fixations, you get to read and understand more words. When you master fixation, you will be able to master speed reading. In today's digital word, a digital method is also appropriate. Rapid Serial Visual Presentation or *RSVP* is helpful when you are reading material on a computer screen such as ebooks, online blogs and articles, and the like.

The RSVP is a speed reading system that allows the reader to focus on one word at a given time as it flashes on the screen. As you continue practicing this system, you will improve the speed with which you can read words on display then speed up the process.

For this, try ***Spreeder*** – it uses the latest innovations to make you more productive and efficient at speed reading. Go to https://www.spreeder.com/ to learn more. It is free.

CHAPTER 9

COMPREHENSION TECHNIQUE: SKIMMING+

Speed reading is more than just getting through a material very fast. It is about understanding the information you have just read better and quicker than you normally would. Speed reading is about efficiency.

Skimming is a skill that is often taught in grade school yet not developed as much. It allows the reader to scan through the content and detect important elements that are to be read. However, skimming does not make you a fast reader, although some people would say it is a speed reading technique.

This is because, as opposed to really reading, you merely scan and skip parts that you decide are not that essential. Usually, skimming allows for little comprehension and you don't always remember every word that you go through. Speed reading is skimming+, meaning it is more than just browsing or gliding through your text.

Skimming+ is all about getting the substance of what you are reading without having to read all the words. People use skimming as a speed reading technique when they have a lot of material to read and you don't have a lot of time to absorb it in detail. Keep in mind that skimming is three or four times faster than average reading so it means that your comprehension certainly declines in comparison.

If you really think about it, skimming is a lot like scavenging because you are looking for the choicest of information, hoping that you don't miss any important ones as you go along.

Skimming also allows you to get a general idea about the text. However, you need to know when you can skim a text and when you should read it in depth. When you choose skimming as your speed reading technique, you should know if the material is worth skimming.

You can skim lengthy business reports or white papers like annual reports or the newspaper. You can also skim through your book when you have an exam coming up and you don't have enough time to review. The key to knowing whether you should skim or not is to answer the following questions:

- *Do you have so much to read and not enough time?*
- *Is it non-fiction?*
- *Can you skip some of the material?*
- *Do you already have a background or familiar knowledge on the material?*

If your answers are yes to the questions, then you don't have to read everything and skimming can be helpful for you.

Here are some tips to properly skim through a material and recognize the essential information:

1. *Identify what your purpose is.*

    Why are you reading what you are reading? When you know the reason, you will know what to look for. You will look out for and find terms that essentially express what it is you are looking for. When you don't know what you are looking for, you will skim without purpose which can be very boring and cause you to not retain many of the information you've just read.

2. *Read both ways – horizontally and vertically.*

   Move your eyes up and down, and side to side. Imagine it as running down the stairs. You are trying to get down faster, but you are also being careful not to miss a step.

3. *Think like the writer.*

   When you do so, you will skip out on unimportant details and just focus on the meat of the material. There is a point that the author is making, and as with number 1 – knowing what you want to get out of the material – you can detect what it is and gloss over examples and stories. It will take practice but you will learn the author's style – how he puts indirect information, secondary arguments and other tidbits.

4. *Find highlights or main ideas.*

Usually, the main idea is written in the beginning paragraphs of any material. Read it carefully so that you will understand the aim of the article. It is also important to read the first sentence of every paragraph. By doing so, you will know if it is worth reading fully and which ones you can skip.

Keep in mind that you don't have to go over the whole sentence if you find that is doesn't have any valuable information. You can skip through examples.

CHAPTER 10

RETENTION TECHNIQUE: MAINTAIN FOCUS

The world we live in offers so many distractions that it becomes hard to maintain focus while you are reading. Steve Jobs says that focus means you are saying no to the other ideas that are coming at you and picking the right one.

In essence, he is saying that focus is more than simply saying yes to one thing. If you do not try to cancel out the noise brought by the other ideas, you will not be able to concentrate on "the one". He stresses that innovation means you decline 1,000 other things.

Here are some simple tips and tricks that can help you keep and improve your concentration which will allow you to have better comprehension as you speed read.

1. *Turn of your notifications on email, instant messengers and mobile phone.*

   You will always feel that you need to check your phone or computer for messages every time you hear that *ping!* go off. You don't have to. These nudges can take your attention away from what you are reading and when you lose concentration, you will find it hard to get back to speed reading.

   You will find yourself having to re-read or you will lose interest entirely. Interruptions can also lower your brain's ability to concentrate on the information you are trying to hold. When you need to speed read, put your phone on silent mode and turn off all kinds of notifications. You can always check them after you read.

2. *Remember that proper posture is essential.*

   Much like how it takes more muscles to frown than it does to smile, you need more energy to slouch that to sit properly. Make sure to practice proper posture when reading.

   o   When sitting, push your hips far back to the chair. Your feet should be flat on the floor.

- Your knees should be a bit lower or at the same height as your hips.

- Get an ergonomic chair – your back should have proper support.

    You will enjoy more benefits than just maintaining focus, you will stay healthy and avoid health issues that come with poor posture.

3. *Clear your mind.*

    You only need a minute or two to do this. Regular meditation will help you a lot because it frees your mind from distractions and mental clutter. While you won't have enough time for proper meditation before you need to speed read a material, you can close your eyes for a minute or two, and release any stressful thoughts or cares that clutter your mind before you read. A relaxed mind will have a higher level of concentration.

4. *Read in intervals.*

    A 50-minute interval is the most ideal time for focusing on an individual task, according to Peter

Drucker. After fifty minutes, your mind will be tired and need a break. When you go beyond that mark, your mind becomes inefficient. You need to take a 10 minute break before you resume reading (or doing any task for that matter). Making this a habit will allow you to train your focus and use your brain at optimum levels.

5. *Read with a purpose.*

When you have a goal in mind, you will not read mindlessly. Reading with purpose will make going through the material easy and fast. When you have a specific goal set in your mind, you will concentrate better.

6. *Find a good place to read.*

Not only should you be in a comfortable, ergonomic seat, you should also be in a room where you won't be distracted by people who might constantly interrupt you. Likewise, eliminate unwanted noise as much as you can.

If you can read while music is being played, then play something easy to listen to. Most people find it not just relaxing to have a background music when doing something, it also helps them focus more. Of course it depends on the kind of music you are listening. Instrumental, classical music or even white noise will do wonders for your concentration.

7. *Make a mind map.*

It is important to work both sides of your brain in order to have better retention. The left side of your brain is for logic and structure while the right side is the artistic avenue. Engaging both while reading will help you retain more information and have better focus.

To train yourself to use both sides of your brain, make a mind map: take notes and draw images. You can first draw a picture of the topic you are reading or want/need to read, then add key words that are connected with it. Your brain will be using both sides as you do this.

When you do begin reading, your mind will just naturally come up with pictures and keywords and help you concentrate more and retain important information.

These are very simple tips but they are very useful and can create a big difference in your reading ability. Be sure to implement these regularly so you can get the benefits of maintaining your focus. You will also steadily improve your reading speed.

CHAPTER 11

KEYS TO SPEED READING SUCCESS

Whatever speed reading techniques you plan to apply, you must always be aware of the purpose of your reading and decide whether speed reading is the most appropriate approach.

When applied correctly and practiced diligently, speed reading can significantly improve your overall effectiveness, as it frees up precious time and allows you to work more efficiently in other areas.

Keep the following in mind:

1. Understanding *why* you should speed read is the start. When you know why you want to do something, it will be easy for you to implement the *how*.

2. Regular practice is essential – you need to make speed reading a habit. Any skill requires

dedication and time. Do not be frustrated when it takes time to improve your speed reading skills.

3. You must break poor reading habits, as discussed in an earlier chapter. After you have done so, you will be able to develop and improve good speed reading skills. No matter how much you practice, poor reading habits can get in the way if you don't break them first.

4. Start your speed reading practice with easy material. If you start with something more challenging, you will most likely fail at it and become disappointed. Work your way up from short stories to a novel after you have practiced one-page or a couple of pages of easy-to-read documents until you become confident.

5. Remember that you cannot speed read everything. There are some things you need to read thoroughly in its entirety and give ample time to comprehend. These include letters from people you love, legal documents,

important financial reports, novels, prose, information that needs to be memorized, and others of similar nature.

6. Learn how to benchmark your current reading speed. Benchmarking can help you monitor your progress. You can find speed reading assessments online.

7. Strengthen your eyes. Your eyes are your primary sense organ for reading so you should make them strong and ready for reading. This can be done through daily eye exercises and rest. The last chapter is dedicated to such exercises.

CHAPTER 12

READ A BOOK A DAY - SPEED READING EXERCISES YOU CAN START AND MAKE INTO A HABIT

Ultra-successful people like Warren Buffet, Bill Gates, John Maxwell, and Mark Zuckerberg believe in the power of reading books. Do you want to be able to read a book a day? As you begin to break bad reading habits that hold you back, you'll start to improve slowly but surely.

Here is a helpful guide to help you take that step:

1. **Wake up decisive.**

    As soon as you wake up, smile and say, "Today is the day I will start learning the techniques for speed reading. And the next days are going to be awesome." Being positive and encouraging yourself will set your mind and focus into achieving your goal for the day: to speed read.

2. **Have a goal.**

   You should decide how much to read every day. You don't have to finish one book in one sitting – but you will get there soon after much practice. For now, you can begin by practicing 10 minutes of speed reading one page a day. And you can increase that as you get the hang of speed reading – you will be able to read two pages in ten minutes the next day, three pages and so on.

   You can also increase the amount of time you dedicate for your daily reading. It can be anything as long as you set a vision before you. Make sure to write smart, attainable goals, especially if you are in the beginning stages of making speed reading a habit. If you make big goals in the early stages of habit-forming, you may get discouraged early.

3. **Choose when to read.**

   Choosing the time you sit down and get to reading is as important as choosing your material.

The key is to know when you are at your optimal reading mood. Otherwise, you will struggle with distractions and feelings of tiredness and laziness.

You can read EARLY every day. Many students do this – they study early in the morning because the mind retains more information in the morning compared to when you stay up late into the night when the brain is tired.

When you wake up every day, do some reading even if it is only for 10 minutes. It will help enhance your concentration and you will be able to train your brain to improve your speed reading rate. *You can also choose to read BEFORE GOING TO BED.* Other people find that their minds are clearer and can be much more focused when they have attended to and completed their tasks for the day.

They can set aside worries and concerns for the next day, so this is the best time for them to read. Reading at night (especially if it's something enjoyable like fiction) is a proven way to relax.

But, of course, you can choose to read ANYTIME of the day. You can read a few pages after you finish lunch still have time before you have to get back to work. You can read during breaks at school. You can read while waiting for dinner to be cooked. You can read while having your afternoon tea.

The important thing: MAKE TIME. Don't out it off till tomorrow or the next day. Do it today.

4. **Get in the right environment.**

It will be quite difficult to read when you are not comfortable. With strained eyes and tired arms, neck or back, you will read at a slower pace, have lesser focus and understanding, and lose interest in reading altogether. Make sure that you get in the right reading environment by doing the following:

- Set up your reading space – one that is free from distractions.

- Get your tools ready: pen, paper, pointer, bookmark – whatever you need to use as a guide or for jotting down notes.

- Use a bookstand so that your reading angle is at 45 degrees.

- If you are going to read from a screen, it is better to use a tablet instead of reading from a desktop.

- Sit properly in a chair. Do not read in bed or while lying down.

- Make sure you have proper lighting.

- Allot at least one hour (50-minute straight reading, 10-minute rest) for reading and only to read and not do (or even think of) anything else.

- Play instrumental music or white noise using a headphone (optional).

5. **Start Reading**

Once you find the perfect reading atmosphere, you can go ahead and start reading. Keep in mind the different speed reading techniques you learned in the previous chapters. You can try one or try them all, but don't do it simultaneously. Choose what works for you.

6. Finish what you start.

Given that you started out with a goal, make sure that you are faithful to complete it. For example, if you decided to speed read for 50 minutes today, do not get up and close your book until that 50 minutes is up. It will take a good amount of self-discipline, but if you stick to fulfilling your goal for today, you will find it easier to do it in the succeeding days and you will form a good habit.

MAKE A COMMITMENT

Make a decision to do this for the next two weeks. Treat it as a "reading appointment" and faithfully attend to it. However, do not consider reading as an inconvenient routine like homework; instead, look at it like an experience that can change your perspective, enhance your imagination and improve other life skills.

Do not pressure yourself to finish one book in one day when you are just starting to build your speed reading skills. Initially, you can practice speed reading for 21 days – the amount of time it takes to form a habit – and follow the reading goal you set. You will build a great reading habit and you will soon find yourself someone who not just reads fast but also comprehends more – a speed reader!

CHAPTER 13

SPEED READING TIPS THAT ENHANCE YOUR HABITS

Good job on starting to speed read!

It will take time and effort and you may get discouraged along the way, but fear not – it is only the beginning and it will get better day by day. Here are some tips that can help you make that speed reading habit stronger:

1. **Use a timer.**

   As you put to practice the speed reading techniques you have learned in this book, it is good to record your time and track your progress so you can increase your reading speed as you go along. Initially, you can set your timer to a minute, then read. When time is up, check the number of pages you have completed. You can get an app that will let you know how many words you read. Make a record your achievement.

Test your skill by doing the same exercise then see how much you have improved by comparing the results. You can set daily goals and start beating your own previous records. To stay motivate, reward yourself every time you beat a record. Turning it into an exciting game also means you won't notice how much effort you put into it and just enjoy the benefits! As you continue to practice the techniques everyday, you will get better.

2. **Use a marker.**

As you learned in chapter 7 and 8, reading fast without a guide can sometimes cause your vision to slip and slide. You may think that you have missed a word or failed to grasp something. There are many things you can use as a marker: your finger, a pen or pencil, a ruler, an index card or a bookmarker.

To use it, place the guide of your choice below every line that you read and glide it down as you continue. Using a marker will help you stay focused and ease your worry of not being able to take everything in. Here is a good exercise:

- For a minute, read a block of text at your regular pace but use a guide. Mark the place where you ended.

- For another minute, read starting from the beginning same text and try to get further than your first time, still using your guide.

- For the third time, read starting from the beginning of the same text and try to read three times farther in the same amount of time, one minute.

- After doing these, check yourself if you can remember what you have read or if you can piece the whole thought together. Go to the next portion and repeat the same practice.

This activity is designed to help you read faster so don't be pressured about recalling information.

As you continue to practice this, you'll get better and better.

3. Make yourself accountable.

As with any goal, accountability helps to ensure that you are sticking to your methods of achieving your goal and keeps you on the right track. You can do it yourself by setting daily reading goals and having a checklist. Once you complete your daily reading requirement, tick it off your list.

You can also have someone check up on you. This doesn't mean that you should be hard on yourself. Give yourself an incentive when you meet a goal, and when you don't, encourage yourself to try harder the next time. Use accountability to motivate and inspire you.

4. Use personal accountability techniques

Dedicate a calendar for your speed reading goals. Hang it on the wall and mark each date with an X or a check mark as you complete your daily commitment. By doing so, you are putting a picture before you of your goal and your progress towards it.

As you see the satisfactory "did it" marks, you will have the motivation to not break your cycle – that is, to read every day. Set smart yet achievable goals to keep you both challenged and inspired to meet them.

5. **Improve your vocabulary.**

    You can practice speed reading all you want but unless you widen your vocabulary, you will find it hard to have full comprehension of any material you read, and it will slow you down.

    Often, you will encounter a word or set of words that you don't know. This will cause you to halt, or skip, or waste time thinking about what it actually means or if it is significant enough. You may find yourself stopping to ponder or look up its meaning. To avoid this, enhance your vocabulary. The more words you know, the easier it will be for you to speed read and you will be able to read and know a whole lot more.

6. **Ask questions.**

You can boost your reading comprehension by checking through headings and subtitles and turning them into questions. This will help you understand what you are looking for when you scan through the text. This is also a good way to increase your reading speed and enhance your focus.

When you know what you are looking for – answers to the questions you formed – you will be more focused and alert to what you are reading.

7. **Preview and jot down brief notes.**

Just like how movies would have a preview, you can get a glimpse of the content of what you are about to read by doing a preview. First, look over the material and find out what is important and interesting. You will also know which ones to skip so that you can focus on what you need to remember.

This will save you time and effort. You can enhance your reading speed and steer clear of re-reading by writing down notes, or making an outline, after reading something. You can use these notes as reference when you need to make a response or a course of action.

8. Do not highlight.

A lot of people use highlighters in order for them to remember important text, thinking it improves their comprehension. It is not true. When you highlight something, you are training your mind to focus on the text that is highlighted, instead of learning the whole material. The problem with this is you may have to re-read the whole thing again since you didn't fully comprehend it to start with.

It's better to speed read – read and understand fully – than to just highlight facts that you deem necessary. There may be information that you have to know that you failed to highlight.

9. Always bring your book with you.

As part of your daily routine, bring your current read along with you so that you can catch up on your reading whenever you find the opportunity; like an unexpected long lunch-hour line at your favourite restaurant or waiting in the bus or subway.

10. Prepare your next book.

Even if you are not yet done with the first one, you can go to the bookstore and choose the new book you are going to read next. When you do this, you are preventing yourself from being stuck without a reading material and feeling sluggish about continuing with your practice. It is better if you can come up with a line-up of books to read for the month.

11. Decide to read, read, read.

Practice always makes perfect. It is true with any skill you wish to learn. Read more and you will become better at it. You can read average-length documents, books, papers, pamphlets, newspapers – anything. Just do it often. This will fuel your goal of improving your rate of reading.

It is also important to remember that you don't have to put pressure on yourself to read what others are reading. Reading should be for your own enjoyment, pleasure, and education. Just because it's the current bestseller doesn't mean you have to get your hands on it because if it is a topic that you won't find exciting, you will just lose interest.

12. **Learn to stop.**

While it is a good goal to finish what you start, you don't have to apply this to every book that you read. Do not feel pressured-- as if you will receive punishment for partially reading a book.

If it's something you don't enjoy, you can close the book and pick up another one. Don't feel bad about it and don't let it become an obsession. As a popular saying goes, "life is too short to read lousy books". More importantly, when your eyes are tired, stop. Do not overexert your eyes or you might suffer injury.

13. **Prioritize reading.**

Often you think that you have so much to do, but have very little time in your hands. But if you make reading a priority, you will soon find yourself having extra time to do other things.

To help you prioritize, you can organize your reading materials into three categories: important, average, and least important. Make sure that you read according to importance. As you read the more important materials first, you will have better focus. Not only will you improve your speed, you will also give more time and attention to things that matter most.

14. Borrow or purchase more books than you can read.

When you are surrounded by books, you will have easy access to reading. When you find a good book in the store, get it. When you borrow books from the library and put them in a pile at home, you will be motivated to read them as you have to return them at a certain date. Having books at home also ensures that you have easily available choices when you do need some reading material.

15. Always do eye exercises.

In the next chapter, you will learn about different eye exercises you can do on a daily basis to strengthen your eye muscles. Eye movement is very crucial in speed reading and when you build your eye muscles, the faster you will read and you will avoid eye strain.

When you make time to practice regularly, you will become a more efficient speed reader. This discipline can even overflow into different areas of your life – you will find yourself learning new things fast and grasping new concepts easily. Don't worry, you can always control your speed! You don't have to feel pressured to speed read all the time.

CHAPTER 14

EYE EXERCISES FOR SPEED READING

Speed reading involves a lot of eye movement. The muscles around your eyes can be strengthened so that you won't strain your eyes whenever you speed read. Exercise will also give you more flexibility and clearer vision. Strong eye muscles will also deteriorate less with aging. Here are some daily eye exercises you can do to make those muscles strong.

1. **Thumb glancing**

    This exercise will stretch the muscles in your eye sockets to make them more flexible and strengthen your peripheral vision as well.

    - Sit or stand up.

    - Stretch both of your arms to the sides. Your thumbs should be sticking up.

- Look straight ahead for a few seconds, then slowly move your eyes to glance at your left thumb.

- Then use your eyes to glance at your right thumb.

- Do not move your head while you are doing this exercise, just your eyes.

- Glance back and forth ten times.

- Repeat the whole activity three times.

2. Resting eyes

This is a good way to relax your eyes, especially when it needs to rest.

- Shut your eyes halfway and do your best not to let them quiver.

- While it is half-closed, look towards a faraway object. You will feel that there will be less to no trembling as you gaze.

- Do this activity two to three times.

3. **Eye-writing**

When you write with your eyes, you are forcing it to move out of its normal fashion, giving you more flexibility. This workout will strengthen the ocular muscles in your eye sockets and give you better range of motion.

- Sit or stand up.

- Look at the wall that is on the farthest line of sight from where you are sitting or standing.

- Picture in your mind that you are writing your name or any word on the wall using your eyes.

- Use your eyes to write your name or any word. Do not move your head along. Only your eyes should be moving like a pen or paintbrush as you "write".

- Write in capital letters.

- Write in small letters.

- Write in cursive.

4. Eye squeeze

These squeezes that involve breathing exercises can help relax your eyes and increase the oxygen and blood flow to the face and around the eyes.

- Open your eyes and mouth wide, stretching your facial muscles, and inhale deeply.

- As you exhale, close your eyes, clench your jaws and squeeze your facial muscles, as well as the muscles in your head and neck, very tightly.

- Hold your breath for the next thirty seconds and continue squeezing.

- Repeat the steps 4 times.

- Take a short 1-minute break

- Do another round of eye squeezes.

- Do this five times.

CONCLUSION

Thank you again for purchasing this book!

I hope this book was able to help you better understand how you can use speed reading to your advantage: read faster, comprehend better, learn more, and be an expert at retaining information.

You have learned the different speed reading techniques and how you can apply them in your daily life.

The next step is to start doing the exercises you learned from this book, ones which will help you create a habit of speed reading. Take that first step and begin speed reading today.

Forget about your initial misconceptions about speed reading and begin to read more efficiently. No matter what level of speed reading you are now, there is always room for improvement. It may take a lot of work in the beginning but remember that you cannot have something significant if you don't put in a significant amount of work into it.

Put your heart into it – excellence is at your fingertips!

Thank you!

Before you go, I just wanted to say thank you for purchasing my book.

You could have picked from dozens of other books on the same topic but you took a chance and chose this one.

So, a HUGE thanks to you for getting this book and for reading all the way to the end.

Now I wanted to ask you for a small favor. **Could you please take just a few minutes to leave a review for this book on Amazon?**

This feedback will help me continue to write the type of books that will help you get the results you want. So if you enjoyed it, please let me know! (-:

Also, don't forget to grab a copy of your Free Bonus book *"How to Talk to Anyone: 50 Best Tips and Tricks to Build Instant Rapport"*. If you want to increase your influence and become more effective in your conversations then this book is for you.

Just go to http://ryanjames.successpublishing.club/freebonus/

Lightning Source UK Ltd.
Milton Keynes UK
UKHW021826061019
351113UK00015B/127/P